THE SIMPLE GUIDE TO

MALAYSIA

CUSTOMS & ETIQUETTE

COVER ILLUSTRATION

'The old and the new.' Sultan Abdul Samad building (foreground) and the Dayabumi complex (background) in the heart of Kuala Lumpur

ABOUT THE AUTHOR

Victor King is Professor and Director of the Centre for South-East Asian Studies at the University of Hull. He teaches on the anthropology and sociology of South-East Asia and has a special research interest in the peoples and cultures of the Malay-Indonesian world. He has written extensively on social and cultural change in Malaysia and is currently series editor for the Oxford Paperback anthologies on South-East Asia, published in Kuala Lumpur and Singapore.

OTHER COUNTRIES IN THIS SERIES

Arabia & Gulf States
England
Holland
Ireland
Japan
Nepal
Thailand
China
Germany
Hungary
Israel
Korea
Russia
Turkey
Czech Republic
Greece
India
Italy
Malaysia
Singapore
Vietnam

ILLUSTRATED BY
IRENE SANDERSON

THE SIMPLE GUIDE TO

MALAYSIA

CUSTOMS & ETIQUETTE

Victor King

GLOBAL BOOKS LTD

Simple Guides • Series 1
CUSTOMS & ETIQUETTE

The Simple Guide to
MALAYSIA
CUSTOMS & ETIQUETTE

First published 1998 by
Global Books Ltd
PO Box 219, Folkestone, Kent CT20 3LZ, England

ISBN 1-86034-011-3

British Library Cataloguing in Publication Data
A CIP catalogue entry for this book
is available from the British Library.

Distributed in the USA by:
The Talman Co, Inc, New York

Set in Futura 11 on 12 pt by Bookman, Slough
Printed and bound in Great Britain by
The Cromwell Press, Wiltshire

Contents

Map of Malaysia 6 Foreword 7

1 A Brief History *9*

2 A Cultural Pot Pourri *14*

3 Festivals & Holidays *19*

4 What to Speak *29*

5 What to Call People *34*

6 Essential Dos and Don'ts *39*

7 Business Matters *47*

8 Eating Out *57*

9 Travel in Malaysia *63*

Useful Addresses 70

Facts About Malaysia 72

Malaysian Words Used In This Book 75

Index 79

MAP OF MALAYSIA

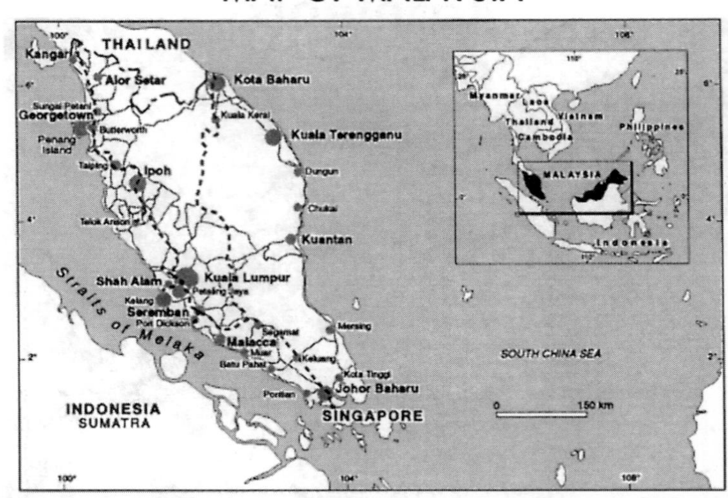

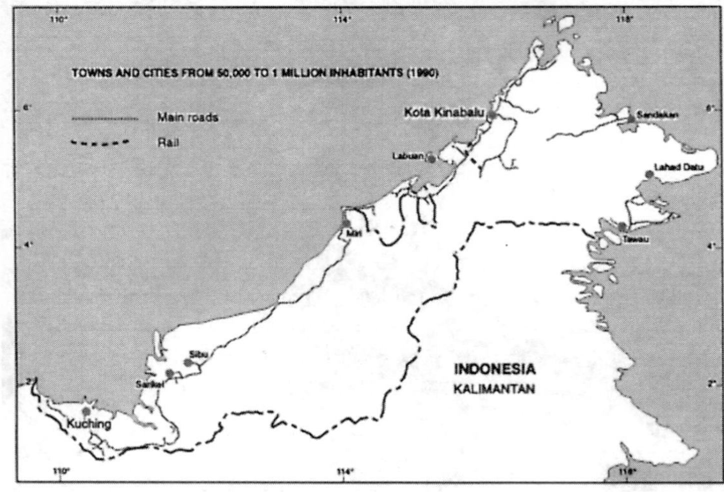

Adapted from Rodolphe De Koninck, L'Asie du Sud-Est

Foreword

Zahir mosque in Alor Setar, Kedah

The Federation of Malaysia is one of the newly-industrializing economies of the Asia-Pacific rim. It is a founding member of the Association of Southeast Asian Nations (ASEAN), established as a regional trading group in 1967, and the looser-knit Asia-Pacific Economic Cooperation forum (APEC). As a predominantly Muslim country it helped to found the Organization of the Islamic Conference, and arising from its British colonial past, it is also a member of the Commonwealth and continues its membership of the Five-Power Defence Arrangement with Britain, Australia, New Zealand and Singapore.

In the space of 30 years Malaysia has transformed its economy from one which relied mainly on small-scale agriculture and the export of primary products such as tin and rubber to one based on modern manufacturing and service industries, including tourism. Nevertheless, it is still a major exporter of agricultural products and raw materials, including rubber, palm oil, tin, pepper, coconut, cocoa, timber, oil and gas. The main development target for the governing national coalition government of Prime Minister Datuk Seri Dr Mahathir Mohamad is for the country to become fully industrialized by the year 2020.

Despite the obvious signs of modernity and rapid change, the widespread use of English, and the evidence of a colonial past, Malaysia still retains much of its Asian cultural heritage. For the foreign visitor on business or vacation the country presents a fascinating and complex mix of different traditions, religions and customs. Indeed, for the foreign tourist a major reason for holidaying in Malaysia is to observe and participate in its vibrant cultures and festivals, and to sample its diverse and exotic cuisine.

This book is designed to help you find your way through this cultural maze and assist you in doing the right rather than the wrong things. It provides a straightforward guide to general behaviour, but it also helps you to a deeper understanding of the most important customs and forms of etiquette by explaining some of the values and principles which underlie them.

Victor King
Autumn, 1997

1

A Brief History

The waterfront, Melaka

The lands which comprise the modern Federation of Malaysia straddle the great sea routes between India and China. For this reason Malaysia, particularly the Peninsula, has long been a focus for maritime trade. Early in the first millennium AD the coasts of what was traditionally referred to as the Malayan Peninsula were the location of small Malay trading states, visited by Indian, Middle Eastern and Chinese merchants. These early kingdoms embraced variants of Indian Hinduism and Buddhism and for a time came under the control of larger states further south in Sumatra and Java in present-day Indonesia. It was not until well into the second millennium that Islam, brought to South-East Asia by Arab, Persian and Indian traders and teachers, began to establish itself.

An important event was the founding of the Malay sultanate of Melaka (Malacca) in the early fifteenth century. It became the premier spice emporium in the region. From here Islam and Malay language and culture spread to other regions of the Indonesian archipelago. The early origins of this ancient culture probably began in the neighbouring area of south-eastern Sumatra.

SPICE TRADE

It was the power and wealth of Melaka, based on the spice trade and the commerce in other exotic goods from India, China and the surrounding region, and its strategic position on the main routeway between India and China, which first attracted Europeans. The Portuguese captured Melaka in 1511 from Sultans Mahmud Shah and Ahmad Shah; the Dutch took it from the Portuguese in 1641, after laying siege to the port-city for six months; Melaka was transferred to the British from Dutch authority in 1824 by which time the ports of Penang (1786) or Pulau Pinang and Singapore (1819) on the fringes of the Malayan Peninsula had been established as British entrepots on the trade routes between the Indian Empire and China.

These three ports were administered together as the Straits Settlements; from 1826 they were a part of British India, then from 1867 the administration was transferred to the Colonial Office. The British were subsequently drawn into the affairs of the hinterland when tin-mining, undertaken mainly by imported labour from southern China, expanded rapidly. A little later, large rubber estates were established, and Tamil Indian labourers were brought in to work on them.

From 1874 Britain progressively concluded treaties with the Muslim Malay sultans of the various states of the Peninsula, four of which (Perak, Selangor, Pahang and Negeri Sembilan), from 1896, were brought into a federal relationship and governed from Kuala Lumpur; the remaining five states (Perlis, Kedah, Kelantan, Terengganu and Johor) were administered as unfederated states with British advisers.

The colonial period saw the large influx of immigrant labour; the Chinese in particular moved into key sectors of the colonial economy, especially in the west coast federated states, whilst the majority of Malays remained as small-holding farmers owing allegiance to their sultans. Malay society and culture continued to flourish in the less developed east coast states of Kelantan and Terengganu. Immigrant Indians performed a range of activities, not only as estate workers, but in trading, retailing, moneylending, the police, army and the professions.

In the Borneo territories of what is now East Malaysia, the British established protectorates in 1888 over three separate states: Sarawak, governed by the Brooke family – the 'White Rajahs'; North Borneo administered by the Chartered Company; and the remnants of the once-powerful

Brunei sultanate. These were the lands of formerly head-hunting tribes, though the coastal regions were mainly populated by various Muslim communities. As a result of British control, immigrant Chinese and Indians also arrived on the shores of Borneo.

It was out of this improbable mix of territories that Malaysia emerged. The nine Malay states together with Penang and Melaka gained their independence as the Federation of Malaya in 1957. Singapore remained as a separately administered territory. The new country was born during a period of turmoil when the British and their local allies were faced with a Communist, mainly Chinese guerrilla movement fighting for independence. The so-called 'Malayan Emergency' began in 1948 and was only brought to an end in 1960.

FEDERATION OF MALAYSIA

Subsequently, the Federation of Malaysia came into being in 1963 when the Borneo states of Sarawak and Sabah (North Borneo) – British crown colonies from 1946 to 1963 – joined with the Peninsula. The Federation is therefore separated between its western and eastern territories by a considerable expanse of the South China Sea. Singapore entered Malaysia but left two years later to establish an independent republic. The Sultan of Brunei, partly to protect his state's oil wealth, stayed out of the Federation altogether.

In the early years of Malaysia the Indonesian President Sukarno attempted to crush the young country during 'Confrontation'; he refused to recognize what he saw as a neo-colonial creation dependent on a continuing British military presence in the region. Sarawak and Sabah bore the brunt of Indonesian aggression. There were also further Communist guerrilla problems in the Borneo territories until the early 1970s, and in 1969 major race riots in Kuala Lumpur between Malays and Chinese after the elections. This was followed by the declaration of a state of emergency, and the government introduced the New Economic Policy (NEP) in 1970 in order to address the economic imbalances between the still mainly rural Malays and the predominantly urban-based Chinese.

This process of economic restructuring has achieved a considerable measure of success, ensuring that the Malays have secured a greater share of the benefits of economic growth and moved increasingly into the modern urban sector. The country has also prospered and enjoyed over 25 years of both internal and external political stability, and generally harmonious racial relations.

Although the issue of overcoming economic inequalities between the Malays and Chinese is no longer such a pressing one, the basic principles of the NEP continue today, in modified form, in the National Development Policy (NDP). The NDP's objectives began to be enunciated from the early 1990s in the Second Outline Perspective Plan; they focused on the importance of sustaining economic growth, encouraging efficiency and entrepreneurship, and promoting industrial and technological development whilst maintaining equality between the main ethnic groups.

2

A Cultural Pot Pourri

Variety in the market-place

Malaysia is a plural society; it is multi-ethnic, multi-lingual and multi-cultural. The total population of the country is currently estimated at just over 20 million, 82 per cent of whom live in Peninsular Malaysia (see map). The majority of the people (about 10.5 million) are Muslim Malays. However, there are sizeable numbers of Chinese (approximately 5.3 million) and Indians (about 1.5 million). There are also minorities of non-Muslim Dayaks in the Borneo territories made up of a large number of different ethnic groups, and aboriginal communities (Orang Asli) mainly in the hinterlands of Peninsular Malaysia; these together number over 1 million people.

Malays and Dayaks are lumped together in the Malaysian Constitution as 'indigenes' (*bumiputera*: literally 'sons of the soil'), numbering just under 12 million people, and they continue to enjoy certain constitutional privileges in such areas as employment, business and higher education. There are also large numbers of immigrant workers in Malaysia from neighbouring countries such as Indonesia, Thailand and the Philippines.

Malaysia's multi-ethnic character is of the greatest significance in economic and political life. Since independence the country has been successfully governed by a national coalition of ethnic-based political parties, at the core of which is the United Malays National Organization (UMNO), which has provided the country with its four Prime Ministers during the past forty years. Other important though junior partners in the coalition are the Malaysian Chinese Association (MCA) and the Malaysian Indian Congress (MIC). There are also numerous smaller political parties mainly representing various ethnic groups in Sarawak and Sabah.

Top Tip: Rotating Kingship

The Federation comprises 13 states, nine of them with hereditary Malay sultans; it is also a political democracy and a constitutional monarchy; the Kingship rotates every five years among the nine sultans when the Conference of Rulers elects one among their number to succeed.

Malaysian national identity is based on the major elements of indigenous Malay culture. The national language is Malay; the state religion is Islam, with freedom of worship for the country's Buddhists, Confucians/Taoists, Hindus, Sikhs and Christians.

Malays are dominant in the main public sector national institutions such as the bureaucracy, police and military. Traditionally, the Malays were rural-based, small-scale farmers, fishing people and traders; many of them also served as administrators in the Malay states. More recently, a rapidly growing urban, educated Malay middle class has emerged, though largely concentrated in the public sector.

The Chinese are mainly in private business, commerce, industry and the professions. Their presence is obvious in the central business districts and markets of the main towns and cities. They are also found in commercial agriculture, such as in market-gardening near urban areas. The Indians are located predominantly in the urban sector in the professions, urban retailing and services, the police and army. Some continue to work in rural areas as estate labourers.

Many of the Orang Asli and Dayaks are still usually found in the interior regions as farmers; some work on public sector plantations and in the timber industry. Increasingly the younger people are finding their way into urban centres working in government and the private sector.

COMMUNITY VALUES

For Malaysians of all ethnic groups the values of family and community are strong, though among the younger generation there is a tendency for these to weaken with the pace of modernization and the physical and social mobility which goes with it. Obviously it is more difficult for urban Malaysians to keep in touch with family in rural areas, though they still do their best.

As you get to know Malaysians you will find that they may attempt to draw you into their circle of family and friends by referring to you with the appropriate Malay kinship term for 'brother' or 'sister', 'aunt' or 'uncle'. The extension of feelings of affection to non-kin as well as the social obligations associated with family is a common feature of Malaysian society.

Malaysians remain very family-oriented and take great pride and interest in their children; small children are lavished with affection, petted and indulged. In a polite way Malaysians will ask you about your own family, particularly if you have children. It follows from this strong sense of social solidarity that individual interests tend to be subordinated to the needs and concerns of the collectivity. In this situation deviation from social norms is difficult. There is therefore a higher degree of conformity than in Western societies, and cooperation and participation in community life are greatly valued.

Top Tip: Importance of Harmony & Consensus

Social harmony is an important part of this ethos. Many Malaysians believe strongly that harmonious relations within the community should be maintained, and that the behaviour, morality and spiritual condition of each person influences others. These attitudes place emphasis on the importance of consensus. Time has to be devoted to consultation with family, colleagues and friends, and to collective decision-making.

Malaysians love committee meetings and the group ethic also finds its expression in traditional Malay village communities with their emphasis on mutual cooperation (*gotong royong*) and consensus (*muafakat*) through meeting and discussion (*mesyuarat*).

Among the Chinese the importance of the patriarchal extended family has also been sustained, and it is still very evident in the family business organization based on kinship, loyalty, and subservience, and the fact that everyone knows their place.

3

Festivals and Holidays

Kuala Lumpur Drum Festival

Given their rich cultural mix, Malaysians enjoy several different religious festivals and public holidays. Islamic, Chinese and Hindu calendars are lunar ones, and therefore the dates of most Malaysian celebrations are not fixed. The constituent states also have their own holidays, usually to celebrate such events as the local Sultan's and/or Governor's birthday. Visitors should check at Tourism Malaysia offices (run by the national Tourism Promotion Board) or state tourist offices for precise dates. The fixed national holidays are:

Worker's Day or Labour Day – 1 May
[the current] **King's Birthday** – first Saturday in June
National Day or **Independence Day** – 31 August

Christmas Day – 25 December.

MALAYS AND INDIAN MUSLIMS

Malays and Indian Muslims are guided by the five basic principles of Islam: the profession or declaration of the faith in God and the Prophet; the offering of prayer, normally five times a day; the contribution of *zakat*, a yearly charitable tribute or tithe; the observance of the fast or Ramadan; and undertaking the pilgrimage to Mecca at least once in one's lifetime.

Hari Raya Puasa

The end of the fasting month of Ramadan, or *Puasa* in Malay, is called *Hari Raya* or *Hari Raya Puasa*, when special prayers are offered at the mosque and open house is held for family, friends and colleagues. Invitations are by word of mouth or on a formal card. It is an opportunity to sample the best of Malay or Indian curries and relishes and varieties of cooked rice. Houses are usually decorated with lights, bunting and tinsel and everyone dresses in their best clothes.

Gifts are not strictly necessary but a nice idea is to take your hosts some flowers, sweetmeats or candy and to greet them with *Selamat Hari Raya* (peaceful Hari Raya). The exact timing of the celebrations depends on the sighting of the New Moon at the end of the month; in the late 1990s it falls in January-early February. Everything shuts down for Hari Raya eve and the next couple of days. The reuniting of kin and friends means that the airports, railway stations, bus terminals and roads are crammed with people returning to their home communities. Usually transport facilities, especially Malaysian Airlines domestic flights, are block-booked several months in advance, and hotel and other accommodation can be a problem.

It is well to remember that there is another Hari Raya for Muslims and this is *Hari Raya Haji*, held in April in 1997 and 1998, to mark the completion of the pilgrimage to Mecca. In some states such as Kelantan and Terengganu there is a two-day holiday with much feasting and celebration.

Weddings

Malay weddings are colourful affairs, and you should accept without hesitation if you are invited to one. Usually the wedding is held in the bride's home and the groom is conducted there in procession, bearing wedding gifts, and accompanied by tambourine beaters and singing. As an invited guest you can send a gift of money in a wedding card, or some useful household item in advance to the bride's home, or discreetly present your gift to a member of the family (often a parent), as they stand in line to greet the guests on the wedding day.

Customs may vary from region to region and can depend on whether the ceremony is held in an urban or rural setting. Bride and groom usually wear richly decorated silk brocade costumes; the bride is adorned in an array of traditional Malay gold and silver ornament.

The main element of the ceremony for the guests, apart from the food, is the *bersanding* (the 'sitting-in-state' or enthronement), when bride and groom sit side-by-side quietly and sedately, with eyes lowered. They are usually seated on decorated chairs on a raised dais, or on a richly decorated divan or bed. Senior family and friends come forward one-by-one to bless the couple.

Honoured guests are often asked to participate in the *tepong tawar* ritual, first for the groom then for the bride. The groom's forehead is touched with a gold-ring, then a dab of rice flour or scented sandalwood paste is placed there, and the head and hands lightly scattered with scented flower petals, and/or rice grains. Sometimes perfumed water is also sprayed over the couple. Older women who gather round the couple will take you through the ritual in the correct sequence and show you what to do with the ceremonial paraphernalia.

After the *bersanding*, the bride and groom turn to each other and feed each other by hand with morsels of sweetened glutinous rice. The wedding feast then commences. The food is either provided in an informal buffet-style, and men and women usually mix and sit together at table. In a more traditional wedding, men and women are seated in separate groups in a prearranged setting. You will be conducted to the table by someone. On departure, guests are normally given a decorated hard-boiled egg in a small container (*bunga telur*), or sweets or chocolates shaped like eggs.

CHINESE

The Chinese are mainly Buddhists and Taoists/Confucians, but we might equally characterize their belief system as a 'folk religion' oriented specifically to the veneration of ancestors. There are three important festivals: New Year; the Feast of the Hungry Ghosts; and the Moon Cake Festival. Chinese festivals are oriented very much to the temples where worshippers burn joss-sticks and present offerings and prayers to the appropriate temple deities. A Chinese household will also often have a family altar at home at which offerings and obeisance are made.

Chinese New Year

At Chinese New Year, which is usually held in January or February and is not strictly a religious festival, business comes to a standstill. It is a national holiday and in most states of two days' duration, the celebrations include street parades and dragon dances. Family reunions are an essential part of the celebrations; food is presented in abundance and many toasts offered. There is open house the following day, with ample supplies of alcohol, sweetmeats and snacks. An abundance of flowers, joss sticks, candles and red oranges decorate the family altar, and families visit Buddhist temples.

New Year is an auspicious time and guests should not talk about anything which is likely to bring bad luck (such as illness, failure, death, and of course politics!). There is the opportunity to pay respects to one's elders as well as have fun with plenty of eating, drinking, gambling, and for the youngsters letting off fire-crackers.

Children are usually given *ang pow* or red paper envelopes containing gifts of money (red is a sign of good fortune). If you are invited to a Chinese home, a gift of sweets, flowers or a bottle of brandy is certainly appreciated. A gift of mandarin oranges is particularly appropriate as a symbol of good fortune.

Hungry Ghosts

The Hungry Ghosts Festival usually takes place between July and August when the spirits of the dead are thought to roam the earth and they have to be fed. They are presented with food and the burning of paper money. The spirits are also entertained with Chinese operatic performances. This is also a time of much lavish eating and drinking. It is especially celebrated among the Penang Chinese.

Moon Cake Festival

The Moon Cake Festival in September, which marks the appearance of the Autumn moon, and celebrates the defeat of the Mongol dynasty in ancient China, is the occasion for the making and eating of a rich pastry – the moon cake. The cake is made from a bean paste, lotus seeds and sometimes duck egg. Colourful lanterns are lit, incense is burnt, and there are family dinners. It is considered an auspicious time for organizing major events such as weddings.

Weddings

A*ng pow* are useful gifts if you have been invited to a Chinese wedding; gifts of appropriate household goods are also welcome. These can be given discreetly to the family greeting party. Normally an expatriate guest would be invited to the wedding banquet; you are unlikely to be invited to the wedding ceremony itself which is usually a family affair. In fact, there are usually two banquets – one hosted by the bride's parents a day or two before the wedding ceremony proper and the other by the groom's parents on the day of the wedding or the day after. Nowadays the reception is usually held in a restaurant or hotel. It is customary for newlyweds and parents to go from table to table inviting guests to drink the *yum seng* or 'bottoms up'.

Other Chinese Festivals

Usually in April-May Chinese and other Buddhists celebrate Vesak Day. This is a national holiday in Malaysia and Singapore; it is a more solemn occasion with prayers at the temple, and marks the Buddha's birth, enlightenment and death. The Dragon Boat Festival is celebrated between June and August and is associated with the death of a Chinese saint who preferred to drown rather than be corrupted. Boat races are held in such places as Penang. The Festival of the Nine Emperor Gods falls in September-October and sees Chinese operas performed, processions, and, at some temples, firewalking ceremonies.

HINDU INDIANS

Hindu Indians follow the ancient scriptures or Vedas. They worship a Supreme Being which has many forms and natures; the most well known aspects or manifestations of divinity are Brahma, S(h)iva and Vishnu. Hindus believe in reincarnation and they hold to a fixed or predestined order of things, which in social and religious terms is embodied in the caste system. Indian households usually have a family altar.

Festival of Lights

The most well known of the Hindu Indian celebrations is Deepavali, the Festival of Lights, which usually falls in October-November. It is the time for the gathering of family and friends to celebrate the triumph of good over evil in Hindu mythology, and the victory of Lord Rama over the evil King Ravana, or of Krishna over the evil Asura. Indian streets and shops are gaily decorated. Open house is held and houses are also decorated with coloured electric lights or lighted oil lamps, flowers, fruits and sometimes floor-decorations made from coloured rice, pulses and beans. It is a time when the old is swept away and a new beginning ushered in, with the hope of good fortune and prosperity to come. People take oil baths and put on their finest new clothes.

Thaipusam

The main Hindu public ceremony is Thaipusam, usually held in January/February. It is dedicated to Lord Subramaniam (Muruga); it is a thanksgiving for prayers answered and also celebrates the virtues of courage, fortitude and endurance. The most spectacular part of the festival is when devotees, who have made a vow during the year past, redeem it by carrying ornamental structures (*kavadi*) attached to their bodies by hooks and steel spikes which penetrate the flesh. The *kavadi* support containers of milk and holy water. Metal skewers can also be inserted through the cheeks and tongue. Participants are in a state of trance while the procession, with singing, chanting, drumming and libations, makes its way to a temple or shrine.

In Penang there are street parades, and ceremonies at the Waterfall Temple; in Kuala Lumpur, the magnificent Batu Caves, which house a Hindu shrine, and are located about 13 kilometres to the north of the city centre, provide the focus of the festival.

Weddings

Indian weddings are similar in form to Malay ones. They are usually held at the bride's house; bride and groom will also 'sit-in-state', and wedding guests sprinkle yellow rice and scented water over them. The wedding feast can be buffet-style or a traditional rural wedding where guests are seated on the floor and are served with curries on banana leaves. During the ceremony prayers are offered to the god Ganesh, a coconut is broken with a cleaver (which symbolizes prosperity, fertility and pureness), the groom hangs a pendant of gold around the neck of the bride, and then the couple walk around a sacred fire. Guests can present gifts of cash in a wedding card, or some useful household item.

CHRISTIAN DAYAKS AND OTHERS

The Christian populations of Malaysia, comprising some Chinese communities and non-Malay indigenous peoples of the Peninsula and East Malaysia, follow the Christian calendar, including the celebration of Christmas. Meals accompanying Christian weddings and other receptions are either banquet-style in a restaurant or held at the home of parents or family. Christmas is the time for the Christian communities to provide open house. Obviously the religious element of a wedding is conducted in church. There are also Easter celebrations, one of the most important being held at St Peter's church in Melaka.

In Sarawak the native celebration or *Gawai Dayak* takes place in early June, when there is much feasting, especially the consumption of large volumes of rice beer, spirits and toddy, as well as dancing and cultural performances in local longhouses. In effect, it is to mark the end of the rice harvest and the agricultural year. In Sabah the equivalent is the Kadazan Harvest Festival held in mid-May. Again dancing, feasting and drinking are the major preoccupations, as well as buffalo races, games and competitions.

4

What to Speak

Traditional shuttered houses

Bahasa Malaysia, which literally means the 'Malaysian language', is the official language and is a standardized form of Malay. With some variations, it is also the official language of neighbouring Indonesia, Brunei, and perhaps surprisingly Singapore. Malay emerged as a language of trade, liberally sprinkled with foreign borrowings from Arabic, Indian and Chinese languages, Portuguese, Dutch and English. To acquire some basic words of Malay is relatively easy, and the pronunciation is not too demanding for a speaker of European languages.

Although Malay has a traditional script called Jawi, which is based on Arabic, the written language has long been romanized; therefore, you can read it, even if you do not understand it. In any case, English is widely spoken in Malaysia and is the language of business and tourism.

Top Tip: Do Not Speak Loudly!

It is not always the case that Malaysians will easily understand a visitor who speaks rapidly to them in a heavy accent and uses colloquial English. Nor does it help to speak loudly to someone who obviously does not really understand what you are talking about. It is advisable and polite to speak clearly, at a moderate pace, using complete sentences.

Given that Malaysia is a multicultural society then many other languages are also spoken in the country, including Mandarin and several different Chinese dialects, various Indian languages, including Tamil, and numerous native languages in Borneo. Yet all Malaysians to varying degrees of fluency will know Malay. However, there are very marked differences between various of the local Malay dialects and these in turn differ from the standard national language.

If you wish to establish rapport with your hosts and demonstrate that you are willing to learn more about them and their culture, then, of course, it is useful to acquire some basic Malay words, including common greetings, and words for 'please', 'thank you' and so on. It is best to buy an up-to-date English-Malay pocketbook. The language is continuously evolving; new words from the international media, especially from the English-speaking business world, are being incorporated and 'Malayized', and transcriptions and spellings can change.

TIPS ON SPELLING & PRONUNCIATION

Here are a few tips on spelling and pronunciation: c is pronounced 'ch' in Malay; therefore *cat* in Malay is not a furry pet, but is pronounced 'chat' and means 'paint', and *cap* is not a flat hat, but is 'chap' meaning a 'brand'. What of other consonants? *G* as in *garam* (salt) is always hard as in 'good'; *h* in *hitam* (black) is soft and usually not pronounced; *kh* as in *khusus* (special) is a hard 'k'; *ng* in *dengar* (to hear) is soft as in 'song'; *ngg* in *mangga* (mango) is hard as in 'tango'; *sy* in *syarikat* (a company) is pronounced 'sh' as in 'shutter'; and *r* as in *baru* (new) is trilled or rolled as in Spanish.

Malay has five vowels like English *a e i o u*; *i o u* are long; *a* is short, and *e* can be unaccented like the 'u' English 'put', or stressed as in French. There are also two dipthongs *au* (as in English 'how') and *ai* (as in English 'die').

Even if you despair of all of this, if you are an English-speaker you are bound to recognize some 'Malay' words which are reassuringly close to their English equivalents. Try these: *bas, teksi, stesyen, kaunter, pos, stem, telefon, doktor, ambulans, farmasi, aspirin, bank, polis, beg, filem, bir, minit*. To make it a little more difficult for the reader the translations of these words have been scrambled in the following list: police, aspirin, minute, doctor, counter, bus, stamp, telephone, beer, bag/baggage, film, pharmacy, taxi, post, ambulance, bank, station, police. Good luck!

BASIC VOCABULARY & EXPRESSIONS

A few common greetings, pleasantries and basic words might also be helpful.

Apa khabar?	How are you?
Khabar baik	I'm fine
Bagus	Good
Siapa nama kamu?	What is your name?
Nama saya. . .	My name is. . .
Darimana?	From where?
Dari	From
Dimana?	Where is?
Kemana?	Which way?
Kanan	Right
Kiri	Left
Selamat datang	Welcome
Selamat pagi	Good morning
Selamat petang	Good afternoon
Selamat malam	Good evening
Selamat tidur	Good night
Selamat jalan	Goodbye, Bon voyage (said by the person staying behind)
Selamat tinggal	Goodbye (said by the person leaving)
Sampai jumpa lagi	Until we meet again
Ma'af	Sorry, Excuse me
Minta ma'af	To beg pardon
Hari ini	Today
Besok	Tomorrow
Semalam, kelmarin	Yesterday
Tidak	No, not

Ya	Yes
Makan	To eat
Minum	To drink
Saya mau	I would like
Beli	To buy
Tidak mau	I don't want to
Saya tidak mengerti	I don't understand
Terima kasih	Thank you
Terima kasih banyak	Thank you very much
Sila, mari	Please (go ahead)
Tolong	Please (request for help)
Minta	Please (request for something)
Laki-laki	Male
Lelaki	Man
Perempuan	Woman, female
Orang	Person
Satu	One
Dua	Two
Tiga	Three
Empat	Four
Lima	Five
Enam	Six
Tujuh	Seven
Lapan	Eight
Sembilan	Nine
Sepuluh	Ten
Sebelas	Eleven
Duapuluh	Twenty
Seratus	Hundred
Seribu	Thousand

5

What to Call People

Souvenir-seller in local costume

The Malay language has a variety of terms to mean 'you', including *anda*, *saudara*, *kamu* and *engkau*, and Malaysians often avoid using them, preferring instead titles and personal names. In informal situations, and once one has got to know the person, first names might be used for address; *kamu* and *engkau* can be used for small children or if you are on familiar terms with the person concerned. Someone of roughly the same age and status could also be referred to as *anda* or *saudara*. Generally an outsider would use *anda*.

However, one is more likely to use forms of address appended to the individual's given name. Malaysians are very polite people and are always mindful of the importance of establishing and maintaining culturally proper relations, which are directly expressed in forms of address. If there is a relationship which is neither too formal nor too informal, then kinship terms may be used; for those in a senior generation *pakcik* (uncle) or *makcik* (aunt) are appropriate, or *abang* (elder brother) and *kakak* (elder sister). For those of the younger generation then *adik* (younger brother or sister) is probably the most suitable term.

Top Tip: Understand Hierarchy & Precedence

Be especially aware of professional or honorific titles which people possess. Usually the most senior title takes precedence. If someone has a title such as Dr or Professor, use it instead of 'you', until you arrive at a more informal relationship. Malay society was traditionally, and still is to a large extent today a hierarchical one, into which the immigrant communities have also been partially drawn.

Royal families, Governors and the Federal authorities bestow honours and titles on deserving subjects. Royalty and the hereditary nobility also carry titles, sometimes a long list of them. Royal status is indicated by such titles as *Sultan*, *Sultanah*, *Tengku* or *Tunku* and *Raja*. One of the most common conferred titles is *Datuk* (a title received from Federal Government or State Governors) and *Dato* (a title conferred by royalty) for a man, and *Datin* for a woman, equivalent to 'Sir' and 'Lady'. If a woman does not hold a title in her own right then she would be referred to as *Tok*

Puan (wife of a Datuk/Dato). Higher titles such as *Tan Sri* (male) and *Puan Sri* (female) and *Tun* (male), indicating a rather more elevated 'Sir' and 'Lady', and *Toh Puan* (wife of a *Tun*) should also be remembered and used.

There are also titles associated with Islam used among Muslim Malays, Indians and Arabs, such as *Syed/Sayyid* and *Sharif* (male) and *Sharifah* (female), demonstrating links with the Prophet. A Muslim man who has been on the pilgrimage to Mecca (*haj*) is entitled to be addressed as *Haji* and a woman *Hajjah*. Other religious titles include *Imam* (leader of prayer at mosque), *Kadhi* (registrar), *Mufti* (religious officer who also assists a judge), and *Ustaz* (a religious teacher).

USING NAMES CORRECTLY

Malay personal names are mainly derived from Arabic, but the same name may be spelt in various ways – Mohamad is a case in point. In Malay society it is a person's first name that should be used; for example, Rashid Abdullah or Rashid bin Abdullah is Rashid the son of Abdullah. He should be referred to as (Mr) Rashid, or the equivalent in Malay *Encik* (Mr) Rashid, if addressing a young man, and *Tuan* Rashid if an older man. A European man is often addressed politely as *Tuan*.

A man's wife has her own name; usually she does not take her husband's name, but this practice is changing. In most circumstances, Naimah Talib (or in its full form Naimah binte/binti

Talib), is Naimah the daughter of Talib. She could be referred to as *Puan* (Mrs) Naimah. However, things are becoming a little more confusing in that Naimah Talib might be referring to the fact that she is married to Talib, and that she is using her husband's name. Careful questioning is needed to establish the name's exact status.

Young unmarried women are sometimes addressed as *Cik*, but this term is becoming a little old-fashioned. *Puan* can also be used as a respectful form of address for unmarried women. Malays also commonly use occupational titles in address so that, for example, a teacher – *guru* – is often addressed as *Cikgu*, short for *Encik guru*.

CHINESE NAMES

The foreign visitor should remember that among Chinese the first name in the sequence is the family name, so that Tan Chee Beng is Mr Tan, and his personal names are Chee Beng. He is not Mr Beng. If married his wife can be called Mrs Tan, but she has her own family name; Tai Ching Ling, for example. She could be referred to as Madam Tai, her first names being Ching Ling. Christian Chinese will commonly have a Christian name and Chinese personal and family names. Chinese names may also be rendered differently according to dialect so that a Mr Goh can also be Wu or Ngu.

INDIAN NAMES

The majority of Indians do not have surnames as such. Someone referred to as B. Siva or Siva B.

would be Mr Siva, this being his personal name. The B. for Bhaskaran is his father's name, and is used in addressing the individual. In official documents he would usually be referred to as Siva s/o (son of) Bhaskaran. His wife, Rajeswary, could be referred to as Mrs Siva, but she too has her own name, and can also be called Madam Rajeswary.

Some Indians are Christians and therefore they have Christian personal names; some also have Portuguese-derived surnames such as Da Cunha, Rozario and Santa Maria.

Top Tip: Recognizing A Sikh Name

You will always recognize a Sikh name: the gender indicator is Singh for a man, with a personal name such as Ranjit, thus Ranjit Singh, and for a female Kaur, with a personal name, for example, Amarjit, thus Amarjit Kaur. A married woman uses her own names, and is not referred to as Mrs Singh, which is, in effect, a contradiction in terms.

Many Dayaks are Christians and carry Christian names, but they also have a personal name, for example Henry Gana. Gana is not a surname; it is a given name. You also find that Dayaks often use a variant of the Malay form, that is the personal name followed by father's personal name so that Jayum Jawan, is Jayum the child (son) of Jawan. He should properly be referred to as Jayum. Sometimes the Malay word *anak* meaning child is inserted thus Jayum anak Jawan.

6

Essential Dos and Don'ts

Tribal carving, Kuching, East Malaysia

WHAT TO WEAR AND HOW TO LOOK

It is an obvious point, but worth emphasis. The foreign visitor should always attempt to dress conservatively unless of course one is at a beach resort, or involved in a sporting activity or forest-trekking. In major towns and tourist spots flesh-revealing attire for women might not provoke that much overt attention, but remember that Malaysia is a Muslim country, and especially in smaller places and rural areas where one is likely to find many more Malay residents, then dressing immodestly is certainly not to be advised. As a general rule, dressing in a manner which exposes too much of the body will bring embarrassment to one's hosts, and potentially to oneself.

In the humid tropics with daytime temperatures usually ranging between 22°C and 32°C, the general rule is to dress comfortably in light cotton clothing. For business meetings or formal occasions, a light-weight suit or a long-sleeved shirt and tie is appropriate for men; rolled-up shirt sleeves should be avoided. Formal appointments usually demand a suit and tie. A smart blouse and knee-length skirt or a long-sleeved dress are suitable for women; trousers should not be worn if at all possible. For attendance at special events such as weddings and receptions, then the appropriate dress is usually indicated on the invitation.

For evening attire, a restaurant meal or a wedding feast it might be specified that men can wear a cotton *batik* shirt. In Malaysia these are usually very brightly coloured and quite elaborately patterned. If you intend to stay for a while in the region or visit regularly then it might be worth purchasing a few shirts. They are very versatile and comfortable in tropical climes. Please remember that neither men nor women should wear all-black attire at Chinese New Year celebrations ; it is associated with death. Nor should you wear all-black or all-white at a Chinese wedding.

VISITING RELIGIOUS SITES

The general rule when visiting religious sites such as temples and mosques is dress conservatively. In any case, there is a specified dress code on these occasions. Remove your shoes on entering a mosque, Hindu or Sikh temple, and, on most occasions, Chinese temples. In mosques which permit women visitors then arms and legs should be covered. Men are not excluded from this prescription.

The manner in which one dresses can be a visible expression of underlying cultural values. Despite the ethnic diversity, the basic principles governing Malaysian behaviour are modesty, reserve and quiet control, and one's costume should reflect these concerns. Do not be fooled by increasingly modern fashions, including miniskirts and tight jeans, worn by young people in towns and cities; there are still codes of behaviour which should be followed, particularly between men and women.

In this connection there should be a brief mention of Islamic fundamentalism. Although the views of the strongly Muslim political organizations have had some impact on Malay society and culture, the Malaysian government has tried to exercise a moderating influence in the interests of maintaining inter-racial harmony and an open economy. Proposals for the establishment of an Islamic state have not been accepted. But there has been a noticeable shift since the 1980s to stricter controls on male-female relations and sexual behaviour, the observation of the fasting rules, mosque attendance and the collection of the Muslim tithe. However, in most cases these changes have not stood in the way of women's increasing involvement in Malaysia's modernizing economy and in public life.

GESTURES, TOUCHING AND DEPORTMENT

Top Tip: Point with the Thumb not the Finger!

The ways in which people move, conduct themselves and use facial and bodily expression are partly culturally determined.

In Malaysia it is considered very impolite to point at or beckon someone with the index finger, or snap one's fingers at someone. The accepted way is to point with one's thumb, bending it slightly with the fingers folded into the palm.

A person can be summoned by holding the hand out, palm downwards and moving the fingers together towards one's body. In short, one gestures or indicates discreetly with the hand and not in a pointed or direct way.

When standing one should not do so with hands on the hips. Again a controlled and ordered deportment is desirable, not one which indicates an impatient, swaggering or annoyed manner. Casual touching in public between members of the opposite sex should be avoided, as should kissing, social or otherwise. One should always endeavour to keep one's hands to oneself when walking out in a crowd. However, you will often see young people of the same sex, boys or girls, walking together arm-in-arm in public. At formal gatherings in Malay and Indian houses you might find that men and women are required to sit separately, and you will be shown your place. Men will normally be seated in a front reception area, and women in an inner room.

If you are in a seated position then do not fold your legs and point your foot at someone, still less should you show someone the soles of your shoes. It is best to keep your feet on the ground. If you have to sit on the floor Malay-style, then do not do so cross-legged, nor should you squat or stick your legs straight out in front of you. You should try to sit with both legs tucked to your side, either to the right or left, with you feet pointing away from your guests.

Top Tip: Shoes Off!

If you are visiting a Malaysian at home, then you should slip your shoes off before entering, unless you are told otherwise. Even if your host does not insist, it will be appreciated if you do remove your shoes. Also remember that respect is accorded, and rightly so, to older people, and you should greet and introduce yourself to them first. Do not stand back and expect them to come to you.

In South-East Asia the head is considered sacred, or at least it is connected with the spiritual domain. This belief is especially strong among the indigenous communities. You should not touch someone's head, and do not pat small children on the head. If you wish to display a sign of affection to a small child then a chuck under the chin or a pat on the cheek will do. Nevertheless, this prescription on head-touching does seem to be declining in some communities.

Table manners are discussed later, but it is essential to remember always to take food offered to you with the right hand; the left hand is considered unclean. If you are paying an informal visit to your host's house then you will usually be served light snacks and drinks. It is best to try a little of everything; you should not refuse food. But if you genuinely do not want something then you should lightly touch the rim of the plate with your right hand and indicate that you have eaten sufficient.

GIFT-GIVING AND TIPPING

The appropriate behaviour and the matter of suitable gifts for weddings and other special occasions, should you receive an invitation, are discussed in Chapter 3. Nevertheless, it is worth repeating here that you should beware of giving or receiving expensive gifts like jewellery, especially if you are on business in the region. Small gifts in cash or kind are most appropriate. Flowers, fruits, and sweets or biscuits, or something special from one's home-country (perhaps porcelain, glassware or a useful household item) are most appreciated.

Gifts of cash are appropriate at Chinese celebrations, and whilst a gift of a bottle of spirits is acceptable to a Chinese, it is not to a

Muslim or a Hindu. Generally speaking, sharp instruments, clocks and handkerchiefs, because of their inauspicious symbolic associations in Asian cultures, are not welcomed as gifts. Usually gifts are not unwrapped in public, and not opened in front of the donor.

Tipping is not required in Malaysia because a 10 per cent service charge is normally added to hotel and restaurants bills. The bill usually has a ++, which also comprises a 5 per cent government tax. However, if you want to reward really good service then an additional tip of up to 10 per cent would be appropriate, and of course appreciated. Leaving loose change behind for a taxi driver or trishaw rider is acceptable, but again not usually necessary. Porters can be tipped a dollar or so per bag carried.

GREETINGS

There are various traditional ways of greeting each other in Malaysia. The strong, pumping male handshake is not appropriate, nor is shoulder- or back-slapping and arm- or elbow-grabbing. Embraces and kissing, however, affectionate and friendly we might wish to be, are not advised either, not even at a wedding. Urbanized Malays, both men and women, will commonly shake hands with you, but it is usually a quite gentle handshake, more of a brief touch than a clasp. Sometimes a man will not be offered a woman's hand, and a nod or a slight bow would then be in order.

Chinese Malays will usually shake hands either between members of the same gender or between men and women. Indian men and women also commonly conform to the Western style of shaking hands.

Top Tip: Learn the *Salam*

Malays might offer a traditional greeting – the *salam*. To respond properly you stretch out both hands together and lightly touch both hands offered by your host. You then withdraw your hands and bring them both to your breast. Using both hands shows respect or deference to someone who, for example, is senior or of higher status. Between equals the *salam* is sometimes performed with one hand, the right hand.

The Indian traditional greeting between men and women is for each person to put his or her palms together in a prayer position with the hands to the chest and a slightly bowed head. A little practice is all that is needed to get it right.

Malaysians also smile a lot, as do South-East Asians in general. You should do so, too, especially when you are greeting them and introducing yourself. But beware – smiles can mean different things. They can simply reflect happiness, goodwill and friendliness; they can express embarrassment and unease, or, on occasion, displeasure. More on this later!

7

Business Matters

Downtown, Kuala Lumpur

SOCIAL AND ETHNIC FACTORS

The Malaysian emphasis on the group or collectivity and, in particular, the trust and respect expected between members of a family and a community also permeate the world of business and commerce. When one recognizes the importance of these values along with the significance of the ethnic factor in Malaysian life, then the business visitor has to be prepared to move deftly and carefully along these sometimes rather tortuous cultural pathways.

Given the importance of collective action the foreign business person in Malaysia has to be prepared to spend time talking with and getting to know potential business partners. Malaysians want to get to know you as a person; they want to know something of your character, background, and status. Malaysians like to do business with those whom they like. Do not expect to reach decisions and conclude agreements and contracts quickly.

Top Tip: Importance of Face-to-Face Contact

Impatience and getting down to business right away are usually not rewarded. Nor is it much use to rely heavily on the fax, 'phone and e-mail. Face-to-face contacts are essential. Even when you have a contract do not place too much store on it. Malaysians tend to seek personal trust and loyalty on a long-term basis, rather than be preoccupied with the legal niceties of a signed document.

Social meetings, dinner together and sometimes an invitation to a person's home (if relations are developing well) are part of the process of building confidence and doing business. These social events provide opportunities to get to know the pecking order and status of potential business partners; who the decision-makers are and who are the subordinates. This enables you to observe the appropriate etiquette of respect and proper conduct in subsequent discussions and negotiations.

CARDS & CREDENTIALS

The business traveller is normally given a business card by his host which contains important clues as to the title and status of the donor. These are a vital part of commercial transactions in Malaysia. The card should be received with the right hand, then held in both hands and studied respectfully and attentively. A card should not be taken casually and immediately pocketed.

Given that so much emphasis is placed on the personal dimension of business relationships then it is important to check out the credentials of potential business partners and their companies. You can easily become the prey of a minority of unscupulous individuals who might offer you contacts and information at a price, and initially provide you with lavish entertainment and gifts.

Tread very carefully in the whole area of gift-giving; bribery is officially condemned in Malaysia. Of course, the provision of good quality entertainment and refreshment in return for their hospitality is expected by your prospective business partners, and they will want to treat you well.

Do not be surprised that Malaysian business operations are frequently based on the close personal, family and ethnic ties of the local elite and on patronage. Prominent Malay ex-civil servants and former politicians, as well as members of the royalty and nobility are often closely interconnected in the higher levels of management and ownership of large state and various private sector companies. In the private sector too, where Chinese interests are firmly located, there are numerous interrelations based on family, clan and dialect group, and influential Chinese and Malay businesspeople sit together on management boards.

Given the dominant position of Malays in government and administration and the Chinese in commerce, the business person chasing a public sector contract or dealing with the authorities will usually have to discuss matters and negotiate with senior Malay bureaucrats. Despite some privatization of public companies in Malaysia, this has been relatively limited in extent. The Malay elite still holds sway. For civil servants such concerns as the national interest might outweigh those to do with pure profit, and political considerations might figure more prominently than commercial ones. Be mindful of the need to observe procedure and take the correct bureaucratic steps.

In private sector negotiations one might also meet with Malay business people as more and more of them have been encouraged by government policy to take up commercial and industrial careers; some have also gone into partnership with wealthy Chinese entrepreneurs. Nevertheless, the private sector, and especially retailing, trade, finance and construction, is still largely a Chinese preserve where the profit motive is usually centre stage, and the ethos is based much more on pragmatism and a flexible attitude towards market opportunities.

The foreign visitor might also be faced with Chinese business people who come across as much more aggressive and shrewd, although these characteristics are still often tempered by the Asian values of politeness, family, community, loyalty, hierarchy and respect.

LOSING YOUR FACE

Westerners are familiar with the notion of 'losing face'. It is an even more important concept in Malaysian society. It is to do with a person's identity, self-respect and honour. It is part of an individual's self-estimation, but it also involves an evaluation or judgement by others in the context of a strong community ethos.

> **Top Tip: Respecting Emotions**
>
> Malaysians, and in particular Malays, tend to be guided rather more by their emotions and inner feelings. Usually these are not openly revealed, but it is as well to beware that this process is in operation, because a Malaysian is likely to be more personally vulnerable in negotiation and argument.

The Westerner generally places emphasis on engaging openly in debate, and in winning the argument by individual skill, fluency and forcefulness. One's emotions are temporarily and deliberately put to one side. Malaysians also recognize this pattern of behaviour, but culturally they are much more concerned with the social context of interaction, and with preserving social harmony. Elaborate codes of conduct are therefore ideal mechanisms for dealing with conflicts and tensions.

Stress is placed on courtesy, humility and deference. No one's feelings should be offended and no one's face undermined in public.

An individual, therefore, should not be shamed. A very commonly used word in Malay is *malu* (embarrassed, shy, bashful, ashamed). It might be used to refer to someone blushing over a personal remark made about them or simply being shy in front of others. But it is usually the consequence of losing face. One feels a sense of shame – one is ashamed – in public. For this reason, the foreign visitor (business person or tourist) should avoid, as far as possible, 'telling it as it is'.

In the West we tend to place a positive value on being open and frank in discussion and negotiation. In Malaysia it is better to be tactful. Compromise is preferred to confrontation. Malaysians are concerned about what their neighbours say and the business visitor should avoid reprimanding, criticizing or humiliating someone publicly. It is considered most rude and thoughtless.

Even if the individual is at fault, confronting him or her with others present and exposing wrongdoing, weaknesses or shortcomings, result in a negative evaluation of your own behaviour. If the person concerned has made a mistake then he or she will feel badly enough about it. Insulting or jeering at someone openly, displaying emotions such as anger or irritation, only result in the perpetrator losing esteem in others' eyes. Least of all should you argue with someone in authority.

Top Tip: Use an Intermediary

A common way of demonstrating your concern or displeasure is through the use of an intermediary, rather than a face-to-face exchange.

Having said all this, it might still be difficult to determine if offence has been given and taken. It is usually through experience that one begins to pick up the subtle changes in manner, facial expression and tone of voice which indicate that all is not well. The Malaysian smile is indeed elusive.

SMILES, NODS AND SILENCES

The sparing of people's feelings and avoiding openly rejecting others and their opinions are important cultural requirements in Malaysia. It is better to be low-key and show due humility rather than be self-assured and pompous. A very commonly used word in Malay is 'sorry' (*ma'af*), and the Malaysian smile is a versatile facial expression with a range of meanings. It can be used to avoid a direct confrontation. A smile and a nod, accompanied by a 'yes' might not be quite what they seem. To avoid open disagreement or offence, they might translate as 'I hear you', 'I understand', but they might not signify that the person agrees with you. Sometimes, they do not even suggest comprehension, but it would be impolite to say 'I do not understand what you are talking about'.

A smile can also signify embarrassment or disagreement, even annoyance. Malaysians do not usually like being put on the spot with a direct question, and there are various devices to cope with this, moving on to another topic, lapsing into chit-chat, and, of course, the smile.

Also, be prepared for periods of silence; Malaysians are not uncomfortable if a meeting lapses into periodic silence; it is a time for reflection and weighing another's position; it can also take the heat out of a difficult situation and restore a balance and calmness to discussion.

BEHAVING YOURSELF

Much of what has been said about social interaction in Malaysia is no more than advising the foreign business person (and indeed the tourist) to be polite and respect one's hosts. Yet there is rather more to conducting oneself in relations with others than being sensitive. If one understands something of the cultural values of Malaysians then adjustment should go a little more smoothly and trouble-free.

In general terms, the art and etiquette of social intercourse is considerably more important in Malaysia than in much of the West. Our stress on individualism contrasts with the greater social awareness of Malaysians. Do not be fooled by things that look familiar, and by the cosmopolitan Malaysian (there are rapidly increasing numbers of them), who speaks fluent English and has lived and been educated in the West. This is advice especially for visiting Britons who will see much in Malaysia which reminds them of the colonial past.

Yet deep-seated cultural differences remain, and most Malaysians will have been born and brought up in an independent, rapidly-changing and forward-looking country to which they have a strong sense of loyalty.

Top Tip: Be Circumspect

For the Briton especially, be circumspect in what one says about the past and certainly for any foreign visitor one should not be too preoccupied by the fact that we do this or that differently back home. Many Malaysians are well aware of these differences and do not need to be constantly reminded of them.

Overall one should not be seen to be interfering. This is especially so in the political field. The importance of the ethnic factor in Malaysia and the problems which this has occasioned in the past mean that the foreign visitor should be wary about commenting on this element of political and economic life. Malaysians can sometimes be very outspoken about their politics but this does not give licence to overseas visitors to do the same.

OFFICE AND BUSINESS HOURS

In general, offices in Malaysia open early at 8.00 or 8.30am, shut for lunch at anywhere between 12.00 to 2.00pm and then go on to 4.00 or 5.00pm Mondays to Fridays. On Friday there is some variation in the hours (see below). Saturday morning is a working period, too, for local offices and companies – between 8.00 or 8.30am to 12.00, 12.30 or 12.45pm. But some international companies have adopted a five-day week. Banks are open weekdays from 10.00am to 3.00pm and on Saturdays from 9.30 to 11.30am. If you are a shopper, then rejoice: department stores usually open from 10.00am to 10.00pm and shops from 9.30am to 7.00 pm or longer.

MUSLIM PRAYERS

Remember that, in an Islamic country like Malaysia, when it is possible to do so, many Muslims will usually pray five times a day, at dawn, midday, mid-afternoon, sunset and after dark. Exact times are subject to seasonal variation. For the midday and mid-afternoon prayers, some larger offices and establishments provide prayer rooms. On Friday when Muslims go to the mosque for prayers, and most of them do, offices usually shut by noon or at the latest 12.15; staff return to work at 2.30 or 2.45pm and go on to 4.15pm; some workers may stay on longer to make up time. In some states – Kelantan, Terengganu, Perlis, Johor and Kedah – the Muslim weekly calendar is followed in government offices, banks and some stores. Friday is the day of rest and Sunday is an opening time.

8

Eating Out

Outdoor eating

You will do a lot of eating in Malaysia whether on business, for pleasure, or both. A common greeting in Malay is '*Sudah makan?*', 'Have you eaten?'. For the business visitor eating together with potential partners is a vital element in building social relationships; an evening invitation to a restaurant or a club is a virtual certainty, and working breakfasts and lunches are increasingly common. The Chinese are particularly keen on doing business at clubs, restaurants and hotels.

COFFEE SHOPS & FOODSTALLS

Malaysians love entertainment and food, and they will be especially pleased if they see and know that you are enjoying their food and hospitality. A common sight is the coffee shop (*kedai kopi*), where breakfast is often taken before the start of the working day and where friends and colleagues can catch up on news. The drinks served are tea, coffee of course, fresh fruit drinks, and a variety of bottled drinks, including bottled beer in the non-Muslim shops.

Equally ubiquitous is the foodstall; these are located in the coffee shops, in hawker centres, and on the open street. They usually offer light snack meals: noodle dishes, soups, rice porridge, dumplings, deep-fried cakes with or without meat, and curries. You can also get rather more ample meals, and many of the food centres with their varieties of stalls are popular family attractions in the evenings. Generally these stalls are clean with good standards of hygiene, but for the first-time visitor it is sensible to be a little wary, and to order cooked food and either hot or bottled drinks.

CHINESE FOOD

In a Chinese restaurant it is a useful skill to use chopsticks and at a Chinese banquet difficult to avoid it. But it is not absolutely essential and you can usually reach for the fork and spoon, utensils which you would normally use in Malay and Indian restaurants. Remember that with chopsticks the bottom stick remains fixed and the top one is mobile. Do not try to pierce morsels of food with a chopstick and try not to get your sticks crossed.

The small Chinese soup spoon is very versatile and can be used for scooping up virtually anything. If you have to dispose of waste food (bones, gristle, fat etc.) then normally a side plate is available for the purpose. Anything a trifle difficult to digest might also be discreetly disposed of on the side plate. If you are not provided with one, then politely ask for it; it is indispensable. If you should want second helpings, then ask for them. Your host will be delighted that you have an appetite and are enjoying the food, but at a banquet you help yourself in any case.

TRADITIONAL MALAY FOOD

In a traditional Malay or southern Indian setting you might be invited to eat with your hands, or to be more precise your right hand (the left hand among Malays and Hindus is reserved for personal hygiene). With Indian hosts you might not only be invited to take food with your hand but also eat it from a banana leaf – main course and dessert.

You will invariably be supplied with a bowl of water or a water vessel (*kendi*) for washing the right hand. Drinking glasses are placed to your left. It is also a good idea to carry tissues with you, a useful supplement to bowls of water. Normally, however, you will be supplied with spoon and fork, the spoon to your right and the fork to your left.

Be prepared to put on weight in Malaysia. Eating usually starts from about 7.30 in the evening; a modest Chinese restaurant meal has five courses, a banquet seven, and a very special meal nine, with lots of Chinese tea. Alcohol is freely available – beer, Scotch whisky and brandy are popular. Your host might well lift out choice pieces with his chopsticks and place them on your plate – a sure sign that you are the honoured guest. Do not refuse! In any case, it is difficult culturally to say 'No' to food offered to you. It is always best to try a little.

With Malay and Indian hosts you are unlikely to be served anything stronger than tea and coffee, usually light fruit drinks. You must also take note of Muslim dietary restrictions; the prohibition against eating pork (it is *haram*, forbidden) and the requirement that other meat must still be *halal* (slaughtered in the manner prescribed by Muslim law). Chicken is usually a safe bet. There is also the Hindu and Sikh restriction against beef. Some Indians are vegetarian, but take milk products; a minority are full vegetarians. There is a wide variety of good vegetarian restaurants in Malaysia.

RAMADAN

In the Muslim fasting month, you can only be invited to an evening meal after sunset. For the business visitor, do not expect to do any deals over lunch during Ramadan. It is forbidden for Muslims to eat, drink or smoke between sunrise and sunset. Business meetings are best held in the morning, and office and school hours are adjusted; there is a shorter lunch break and earlier closing hours.

Top Tip: Respect for Ramadan

It is not appropriate to take food or drink in the presence of someone who is fasting, and rather thoughtless to ask whether or not they are fasting.

Outside of daylight hours it is also a busy time for women who are preparing food in the restricted hours of evening and early morning. It is best not to call casually at a Muslim home during this time.

Malay food is generally hotter than Chinese, with a wide variety of curried and spicy dishes; common additions to Malay food are fermented prawn paste or *belachan*, turmeric, cloves, anise, chilli, pepper, cumin, caraway and fenugreek. Coconut cream is used copiously. If invited to eat out your host will usually order a variety of dishes along with rice, but will often ask if you have particular favourites and whether or not you can take spicy food. For someone who finds chilli a problem there are many delicious mild meat, fish and vegetable side-dishes from which to choose.

Do not assume that only one dish is for you; the idea is to take a little from the many different foods on offer. The Western palate is now rather more accustomed to curried dishes, especially from India, and there is an excellent range of Indian food available in Malaysia.

If you are the guest for the night out then you would not expect to pay, nor would you go shares. The bill is met by the host. However, you can always reciprocate at some later date, but you should seek advice on where to take your guests and ensure that you know what their religion is and the food permitted and forbidden to them.

A RICH VARIETY

If you do like experimenting with food, then you will have many hours of enjoyment in Malaysia. Many foreign visitors are familiar now with Malay *sate/satay*, skewered grilled meat, with a dip of peanut sauce; *nasi lemak* is a must – rice garnished with spicy sauce, chicken, peanuts, anchovies, half a boiled egg and slices of cucumber; as is *nasi campur* – rice with a selection of meats and sauce, and beef *rendang* – meat long simmered in spices, chillies and coconut milk until relatively dry.

Chinese cuisine is now known the world over and there are superb restaurants in Malaysia with excellent standards. Or just try Chinese noodles (*mee*) with soup or Chinese snacks (*dim sum*), which usually comprise dumplings, rolls, puffs filled with meat, prawns and fish, and spicy spare ribs. For the gourmet shark's fin, turtle eggs, sea cucumber and birds' nests are worth a taste, as is *Nonya* cooking, characteristic of the long-settled Chinese communities of Penang and Melaka, which provides a delightful local blend of Chinese and Malay cuisine. Indian griddle cakes (generally called *roti*) have to be tried; they come in all shapes, sizes and textures. A favourite is *roti chanai* with a pea or lentil curry sauce.

9

Travel In Malaysia

Enjoying jungle scenery by boat

In general, the country has a very good transport infrastructure, but there are four basic matters to bear in mind when travelling.

CLIMATE

Variations in climate can affect certain kinds of travel at certain times of the year. Although Malaysia has a relatively even rainfall throughout the year, the north-east monsoon can be especially severe on the east coast of the Peninsula from October/November through to January/February and along the north-east coasts of Borneo from October to April in Sarawak and up to February in Sabah. Heavy rains, high winds and flooding can occur in exposed regions. Some peninsular east coast resort facilities might close down for a time during the monsoon period, and boat services are sometimes disrupted.

ON FOOT

For the foreign visitor unused to a humid tropical climate it is not advisable that you pound around the towns and countryside on foot, or certainly not until you have become acclimatized. Depending on your state of physical health you might find that short walks in town for sightseeing and shopping are all that you can tolerate, interspersed with moments of respite in an air-conditioned shopping-mall, restaurant or taxi.

You should try to plan your itineraries carefully, allow plenty of time and be sure that you can get to a taxi or bus if you need to get out of the sun and off your feet. For the fair-skinned, sunblocks, hats and umbrellas are useful; an umbrella protects against the sun and the sudden heavy tropical downpour; and covering one's shoulders and arms when walking in town is not just a way of ensuring one's modesty. If you are on foot in town, then use pavements, underpasses and overpasses; some Malaysian drivers, whilst they do have some self-control, can be a bit unpredictable.

Despite the hazards of walking, it is far more sensible than going on a bike (motorized or otherwise), unless you are very adventurous, fearless in traffic, extremely fit, and fully protected against the sun. If you are a bike enthusiast then you could hop into a rickshaw; they are gradually disappearing from the streets of Malaysia, but still numerous in such places as Georgetown in Penang. They provide a leisurely way of seeing street-life in the cool of the early evening.

MAPS

Maps in Malaysia are not that good, but they are improving. Tourist street maps of the main cities and towns, especially Kuala Lumpur, Penang and Melaka are usually serviceable, but often not that detailed. For smaller places you sometimes need to take a chance and follow your nose. There are good road maps, but the best are produced by foreign publishers.

DISTANCES

Malaysia is a relatively large country and is divided into two parts separated by a substantial expanse of the South China Sea. If you wish to see as much of the country as possible during your stay you will probably end up taking domestic flights, particularly if you are on a two- or three-resort holiday which includes both the Peninsula and Malaysian Borneo. Although infra-structure is good in comparison with some other parts of South-East Asia, getting around does take time, and if you want to visit rather more remote places in Sarawak or Sabah, for example, then do allow for possible delays on roads or along rivers.

TRANSPORT

You are spoiled for choice. In towns taxis are a good bet. They are usually air-conditioned. In peninsular Malaysia they are metered and reasonably priced, but make sure the driver switches the meter on; tourists are easy prey to taxi-drivers who try to charge an inflated fixed rate. In Sarawak and Sabah, taxis are not metered and are more expensive; agree the fare with the driver in advance. You are well advised to take a map, and a pen and paper with you. Although you can usually make yourself understood, you do on occasion meet blank stares or end up in totally the wrong destination.

Top Tip: Take A Charter Taxi

A wonderful innovation is the long-distance charter taxi. These are usually located at stands near bus stations or in other prominent locations. The driver waits until he gets four passengers; rates are very reasonable indeed. If you do not wish to wait for a full load, then you have to pick up the remaining fares. You can usually travel in comfort, but it depends on the driver, some of whom travel at hair-raising speeds and overtake on blind corners.

You can also take the long-distance air-conditioned express buses which are also very reasonably priced. Town buses are fun, and you should experience them, but they can be very crowded, noisy and uncomfortable. In Kuala Lumpur, the mimibuses are convenient and numerous, but because they are smaller and more manoeuvrable than ordinary buses, drivers often have a very flexible notion of where a bus-stop is.

Car Rental

If you want to drive yourself then there are many car-rental agencies in Malaysia, both international companies like Avis and Hertz, and local firms. You should check out the special three-day and weekend rates and take out the appropriate additional insurance. Malaysians drive on the left; drivers and front passengers must wear seat-belts.

If you are going to explore off the beaten track, especially in Sarawak and Sabah, then four-wheel drive vehicles are essential. On the Peninsula there is a very good road network, with the tolled superhighway running from the Thai border via Kuala Lumpur to Singapore. Near major urban and industrial centres roads are busy and often clogged with slow-moving heavy vehicles. Try to avoid Kuala Lumpur in the morning and evening rush-hours; traffic jams in the capital are legendary.

Railways

For the romantic traveller a railway journey is a must. The rail network is operated by the privatized national railway company, Keretapi Tanah Melayu (KTM), and the main line runs all the way from Singapore to Kuala Lumpur, Butterworth (Penang) and on to the Thai border, with a number of branch lines.

There are three services: express with air-conditioning and usually first- and second-class; limited express which is somewhat slower, with some air-conditioning, but with third-class available as well; and the stop-anywhere, non-air-conditioned local trains (if you have a few days to spare and want to see the countryside). There is also a short stretch of railway in Sabah, which runs from Kota Kinabalu to Beaufort and Tenom; the western end of the journey runs through the spectacular scenery of the Crocker Range.

Boats

In Malaysian Borneo, aside from road- and air-travel you are likely to end up on a boat. Given that the road system is still not extensive, there continues to be heavy reliance on river transport, particularly if you are travelling into the interior. On the major rivers there are regular express-boat services, with relatively low fares and on-boat video and musical entertainment. It is a good way to catch glimpses of jungle scenery and local longhouse communities.

Planes

But if you just want to get from one place to another fast, and take in the major sights and resorts, then it is air-travel, probably on the domestic carrier, Malaysian Airlines. It serves all major towns and cities, and, using small planes, some out-of-the way places as well. There are regular shuttle services between Singapore and Kuala Lumpur operated by both Malaysian and Singapore Airlines. You can also get some cheap deals on Malaysian Airlines with the Discover

Malaysia Pass, provided you have used the airline to enter the country, and other discounted tickets, for evening travel for example. The airline is generally efficient, but do reconfirm domestic flights at least 24 hours in advance (overbooking is a problem, especially at holiday times), and beware the cancellations at short notice. Other international airlines serve various destinations in Malaysia, outside of the capital, including Penang, Kuching and Kota Kinabalu.

SHOPPING & SIGHTSEEING

Malaysia is the ideal place to shop for a large range of consumer goods, at least in the main towns and cities of the Peninsula, and particularly Kuala Lumpur. Sarawak and Sabah tend to be more expensive than West Malaysia. If you are a lazy shopper for handicrafts then you should go to the standard government craft centres. You will find a good range of products on sale but at tourist prices. If you want to shop around, then there are many small shops selling locally produced items, though you might have to bargain. Even so prices are generally much more reasonable.

Obvious local goods to go for are Malaysian batiks, Selangor pewter, woven cloths from Sarawak, and a range of indigenous crafts from Malaysian Borneo, including rattan baskets, wood carvings and beadwork. Casual shopping in local Chinatowns can often reveal a wealth of locally woven baskets, containers, and hats which provide ideal souvenirs and gifts.

Useful Addresses

MALAYSIAN MINISTRIES

Prime Minister's Department, Jalan Dato Onn, 50505 Kuala Lumpur, Tel: (03) 232-1957

Ministry of Agriculture, Wisma Tani, Jalan Sultan Salahuddin, 50624 Kuala Lumpur, Tel: (03) 298-2011

Ministry of Culture, Arts and Tourism, 34-36th Floor, Menara Dato Onn, Putra World Trade Centre, 50694 Kuala Lumpur, Tel: (03) 293-7111

Ministry of Defence, Jalan Padang Tembak, 50634 Kuala Lumpur, Tel: (03) 292-1333

Ministry of Domestic Trade and Consumer Affairs, Block 10, Kompleks Pejabat Kerajaan, Jalan Duta, 50622 Kuala Lumpur, Tel: (03) 254-6022

Ministry of Education, Block J, Pusat Bandar Damansara, 50604 Kuala Lumpur, Tel: (03) 255-6900

Ministry of Finance, Block 9, Kompleks Pejabat Kerajaan, Jalan Duta, 50592 Kuala Lumpur, Tel: (03) 254-6066

Ministry of Foreign Affairs, Wisma Putra, Jalan Wisma Putra, 50602 Kuala Lumpur, Tel: (03) 248-8088

Ministry of Health, Jalan Cenderasari, 50590 Kuala Lumpur, Tel: (03) 298-5077

Ministry of Home Affairs, Jalan Dato Onn, 50546 Kuala Lumpur, Tel: (03) 230-9344

Ministry of Information, Angkasapuri, Bukit Putra, 50610 Kuala Lumpur, Tel: (03) 282-5333

Ministry of International Trade and Industry, Block 10, Kompleks Pejabat Kerajaan, Jalan Duta, 50622 Kuala Lumpur, Tel: (03) 254-0033

Ministry of Primary Industries, 6-8th Floors, Menara Daya Bumi, Jalan Sultan Hishamuddin, 50654 Kuala Lumpur, Tel: (03) 274-7511

Ministry of Public Enterprises, 3rd Floor, Wisma PKNS, Jalan Raja Laut, 50652 Kuala Lumpur, Tel: (03) 298-5022

Ministry of Rural Development, 5th Floor, Kompleks Kewangan, Jalan Raja Laut, 50606 Kuala Lumpur, Tel: (03) 291-0255

Ministry of Science, Technology and the Environment, 14th Floor, Wisma Sime Darby, Jalan Raja Laut, 50662 Kuala Lumpur, Tel: (03) 293-8955

Ministry of Transport, 5-7th Floors, Wisma Perdana, 50616 Kuala Lumpur, Tel: (03) 254-8122

OTHER ORGANIZATIONS

Tourist Development Corporation of Malaysia, 24-27th Floors, Putra World Trade Centre, Jalan Tun Ismail, 50480 Kuala Lumpur, Tel: (03) 293-5188

Associated Chinese Chambers of Commerce and Industry of Malaysia, 8th Floor, Office Tower Plaza Berjaya, 12 Jalan Imbi, 55100 Kuala Lumpur, Tel: (03) 245-2503

Malay Chamber of Commerce and Industry, Kuala Lumpur, Tel: (03) 433090

Malaysian Associated Indian Chambers of Commerce and Industry, 116 Jalan Tuanku Abdul Rahman, 50100 Kuala Lumpur, Tel: (03) 292-4817

Facts About Malaysia

The two main territories of Malaysia – the peninsula or West Malaysia and Malaysian Borneo (Sarawak and Sabah) – are separated from each other by 640 km of sea.

Malaysia has a total land area of 329,747 sq km and a population of about 20,000,000. The majority of the population (about 82%) live on the Peninsula.

Major Cities

The capital of Malaysia is Kuala Lumpur, situated in West Malaysia. Other major cities on the Peninsula include Penang, Johor and Melaka, while in East Malaysia, major cities are Kuching in Sarawak and Kota Kinabalu in Sabah.

East Malaysia accounts for about 60% of the total land area, being approximately 1,070 km long and 250 km wide at maximum. A coastal plain, between 16 and 64 km wide, borders the mountainous interior of the island of Borneo, at the heart of which runs the border between East Malaysia and Indonesia in the south of the island. Peaks in Sabah, the most mountainous of the two territories of East Malaysia, reach on average 1200 to 2000m, although Mount Kinabalu soars to 4101m, and is the highest peak in South-East Asia.

West Malaysia is about 800 kms long and 300 kms at its widest point, and dominated by a series of mountain ranges which have led to settlement and development taking place primarily along the western coastal fringe which extends up to 80 kms inland in places.

Sarawak has some of the largest natural cave systems and underground passageways in the world at Gunang Mulu not far from Niah. The earliest evidence of human settlement in South East Asia was uncovered when a human skull was discovered in the Niah limestone cave complex during excavations in the 1950s and was dated as over 35,000 years old.

Religious Celebrations, National Holidays and Festivals

New Year's Day	January 1
Chinese New Year – January or February	
Hari Raya Puasa – January-February (the end of Ramadan, a three day festival)	
Vesak Day – April or May	
Labour Day	May 1
King's Birthday	June 5
Birthday of the Prophet – July or August	
National Day	August 31
The Moon Cake Festival – around September	
Deepavali – October/November	
Christmas Day	December 25

For the ten years up to 1997, Malaysia's economy enjoyed average annual growth rates of over 8 per cent, confirming its position as a newly industrializing country on the threshold of developed status.

From being a world exporter of rubber and tin during the colonial period Malaysia has become a world leader in the manufacture of semi-conductors, air-conditioning units and rubber gloves. A third of Malaysia's Gross Domestic Product is now provided by manufacturing industry and half its exports by value comprise electronics and electrical machinery. Malaysia has been producing automobiles since 1985, and its national car, the Proton, is now exported to many countries, including Britain.

Business hours vary from state to state. As a general rule the hours are 8.00am to 12.45pm and 2.00pm to 4.15pm, Monday to Friday, and 8.00am to 12.45pm on Saturday.

Shops are usually open between the hours of 9.30am-7.00pm although some department stores might open until 9.00 or 10.00pm.

Post Offices usually open between 8.00am and 5.00pm Monday to Friday, and between 8.00am and 12 noon on Saturdays.

Public telephones are widespread and take coins and telephone cards, although there are two separate systems in operation which take different cards.

Climate

Malaysia has a tropical climate and is hot and humid all year round. Humidity averages 85-90%. The temperature varies little across the country with a year-round high of about 32 degrees C, with a low of around 23 degrees C. The average number of days of rain per month is shown below.

	Jan	Feb	Mar	Apr	May	Jun	Jul	Aug	Sep	Oct	Nov	Dec
Kuala Lumpur	14	14	17	20	16	13	12	14	17	20	20	18
Kota Kinabalu	9	11	10	15	19	16	15	17	18	21	21	19

Malaysian Currency

Malaysian currency is the ringgit (RM), also known as the Malaysian dollar, which is equal to 100 sen. The denominations are RM1000, RM500, RM100, RM50, RM20, RM10, RM5 and RM1 notes and RM1, 50 sen, 20 sen, 5 sen 1sen coins. Credit cards are widely accepted in hotels, restaurants and major shops, and the banks are very efficient, many with automated cash machines that accept major credit cards.

English language newspapers are available in the larger towns, especially *The New Straits Times*.

Malaysian Words Used In This Book

(page references in italics)

abang	elder brother 35
adik	younger brother, sister 35
ambulans	ambulance 31
anak	child (of) 38
anda	you 34
ang pow	red packet containing cash (a gift) 24, 25
apa?	what? 32
apa khabar?	how are you? 32
aspirin	aspirin 31
bagus	fine 32
bahasa	language 29
baik	good, well 32
bank	bank 31
banyak	much, many 33
baru	new 31
bas	bus 31
batik	patterned cloth 40
belachan	prawn/fish paste 61
beli	to buy 33
bersanding	sit ceremonially on a dais 22
besok	tomorrow 32
bir	beer 31
bumiputera	native, indigene 15
bunga telur	decorated egg (as a gift at a wedding) 22
cap	brand, stamp, seal 31
cat	paint 31
darimana?	from where? 32
datang	to come 32

dengar	to hear 31
dimana?	where? 32
dim sum	Chinese snacks/'cakes' 62
doktor	doctor 31
dua	two 33
duapuluh	twenty 33
empat	four 33
enam	six 33
engkau	you 34
garam	salt 31
gawai Dayak	festival 28
gotong royong	mutual help/cooperation 18
guru	teacher 37
haj	pilgrimage 36
halal	permitted (under Muslim law) 60
haram	forbidden (under Muslim law) 60
hari	day 32
hari ini	today 32
hitam	black 31
imam	leader of prayer at mosque 36
jalan	path, road, travel 32
kadhi	Muslim registrar 36
kakak	elder sister 35
kamu	you 32, 34
kanan	right 32
kavadi	Hindu ornamental load/structure 27
kedai kopi	coffee house 58
kelmarin	yesterday (before dark) 32
kemana?	which way? 32
kendi	water vessel 59
khusus	special 31

kiri	left 32
laki-laki	male 33
lapan	eight 33
lelaki	man 33
lima	five 33
ma'af	sorry, forgiveness 32, 53
makan	to eat 33, 57
makcik	aunt 35
malam	night 32
malu	ashamed, shy 52
mangga	mango 31
mari	come, come here 33
mau	to want, wish 33
mengerti	to understand 33
mesyuarat	meeting 18
mee	Chinese noodles 62
minit	minute 31
minta ma'af	Beg pardon 32
minum	to drink 33
muafakat	consensus, agreement 18
mufti	Muslim jurist 36
nama	name 32
nasi	cooked rice 62
nasi campur	mixed rice/meat dish 62
nasi lemak	spicy rice-based dish (buttered rice) 62
orang	person 33
pagi	morning 32
pakcik	uncle 35
perempuan	woman, female 33
petang	afternoon, evening 32
rendang	dry meat curry with coconut milk 62
roti	bread 62
roti chanai	Indian griddle cake 62
salam	greeting, peace 46
sampai jumpa lagi	until we meet again 32

sate/satay	grilled skewered meat 62
satu	one 33
saudara	you 34
saya	I 32, 33
sebelas	eleven 33
selamat	peaceful, safe, good. . . 20, 32
semalam	yesterday 32
sembilan	nine 33
sepuluh	ten 33
seratus	hundred 33
seribu	thousand 33
siapa?	who? 32
sila	please 33
siapa nama kamu?	what is your name? 32
stem	stamp 31
stesyen	station 31
sudah	already 57
syarikat	company 31
telefon	telephone 31
tepong tawar	wedding blessing 22
terima kasih	thank you 33
tidak	no, not 32, 33
tidur	to sleep 32
tiga	three 33
tinggal	to depart, live, stay 32
tolong	to help 33
ustaz	religious teacher 36
ya	yes 33
yum seng	Chinese toast 25
zakat	Muslim tithe 20

Index

address 34-38
alcohol 24, 28, 60
Arabs 10

banks 74
Batu Caves 27
Beaufort 68
body language 42-43, 45-46, 53-54
Borneo (see Sarawak, Sabah)
bribery 44, 49
Brooke family 11
Brunei 12
Buddhism 9, 23-25
business 47-56, 74
  cards 47-49
  decision-making 48
  hours 55-56, 74
  negotiations 48, 50, 51-52
  organization 49
  partners 48, 49

Chartered Company 11
Chinese 9, 11-13, 16, 18
  festivals 23-25
  food 23, 24, 25
  names 37
  trade 9-10
  weddings 25
Chinese New Year 23-24
chopsticks 58
Christianity 28, 38
climate 40, 63-64, 74
clothes 39-41, 43
coffee shops 57-58
Confrontation 12-13
Confucianism 23
Crocker Range 68
curries (see food)

Dayaks 14, 16, 28, 38
Deepavali 26
Dragon Boat Festival 25

economy 10, 11, 13, 73
ethnicity, ethnic issues 13, 14-16, 47, 50

'face' 51-53
family organization 17-18
Five-Power Defence Arrangement 7
food 57-62
  eating out 57-62
  prohibitions 60
  types of 58, 60, 61, 62

Georgetown (see Penang)
gifts 44-45, 49, 69
  acceptance of 44
  giving 21, 24
  types of 21, 24
greetings 45-46

Hari Raya Haji 21
Hari Raya Puasa 20-21
Hinduism 9, 26-28
Hungry Ghosts Festival 24

Indians 9, 11, 16
  festivals 26-28
  food 27
  names 37-38
  weddings 27-28
invitations 20, 21, 24, 25
Islam 9-10, 20-22, 36, 39

Johor 11, 56, 72

Kedah 11, 56
Kelantan 11, 21, 56
Keretapi Tanah Melay (KTM) 67-68

Kinabalu 72
kingship 15
Kota Kinabalu 68, 69, 72
Kuala Lumpur 11, 13, 27, 67, 68, 69, 72
Kuching 69, 72

language 29-38
English 30, 74
Malay 29-37
pronunciation 31-32
use of 30, 34-37

Mahathir Mohamad (Datuk Seri Dr) 8
Malaya 12
Malayan Emergency 12
Malays 11-13, 16, 18
festivals 20-22
food 22, 59-60
names 36-37
weddings 21-22
Malaysian Airlines 21, 68-69
Malaysian Chinese Association (MCA) 15
Malaysian Indian Congress (MIC) 15
Melaka (Malacca) 10, 28, 62, 72
Moon Cake Festival 24

Negeri Sembilan 11
Niah 72-73
Nonya cooking 62

Pahang 11
patronage 49
Penang (Pulau Pinang) 10, 24, 25, 27, 62, 65, 67, 69, 72
Perak 11
Perlis 11, 56
politeness 54-55
politics 55
public holidays 19-20, 73

religion 19-28
royalty 15, 35-36

Sabah (North Borneo) 11, 12, 28, 63, 65, 66, 67, 72-73
Sarawak 11, 12, 28, 63, 65, 66, 67, 72-73
Selangor 11
shame 51-52
shopping 69
Sikhism 38
Singapore 12, 67, 68
social status 48-49
souvenirs 69
spices 10, 61
Straits Settlements 10
Sukarno 12-13
Sultan Ahmad Shah 10
Sultan Mahmud Shah 10
sultanates 10, 11, 35

table manners 44, 58-62
Tamils 11
Taoism 23
temples 41
Tenom 68
Terengganu 11, 21, 56
Thaipusam 26-27
tipping 45
transport 66-69
airlines 68-69
boats 68
buses 66-67
car rentals 67
railways 67-68
rickshaws 64-65
taxis 66

United Malays National Organization (UMNO) 15

Vesak Day 25

Waterfall Temple 27